Executive Summary

Lightning over Water

Sharpening America's Light Forces for Rapid Reaction Missions

John Matsumura

Randall Steeb

John Gordon

Russell Glenn

Tom Herbert

Paul Steinberg

Prepared for the
United States Army and the Office of the Secretary of Defense

RAND
Arroyo Center • NDRI

The research described in this report was sponsored by the United States Army and by the Office of the Secretary of Defense (OSD). The research was conducted in RAND's National Defense Research Institute, a federally funded research and development center supported by the OSD, the Joint Staff, the unified commands, and the defense agencies under Contract DASW01-95-C-0059, and in RAND Arroyo Center, a federally funded research and development center sponsored by the United States Army under Contract No. DASW01-96-C-0004.

Library of Congress Cataloging-in-Publication Data

Lightning over water: sharpening America's light forces for rapid reaction missions—
executive summary / John Matsumura ... [et al.].
    p. cm.
    "MR-1196/1-A/OSD."
    ISBN 0-8330-2947-9
    1. United States. Army. Infantry. 2. Light infantry—United States. 3. United
States. Army—Airborne troops. I. Matsumura, John.

UD160 L57 2000
355'.033273—dc21

                                    00-036920

RAND is a nonprofit institution that helps improve policy and decisionmaking through research and analysis. RAND® is a registered trademark. RAND's publications do not necessarily reflect the opinions or policies of its research sponsors.

Published 2001 by RAND
1700 Main Street, P.O. Box 2138, Santa Monica, CA 90407-2138
1200 South Hayes Street, Arlington, VA 22202-5050
RAND URL: http://www.rand.org/
To order RAND documents or to obtain additional information,
contact Distribution Services: Telephone: (310) 451-7002;
Fax: (310) 451-6915; Internet: order@rand.org

Preface

SINCE THE END OF THE COLD WAR, the U.S Army has largely been operating in a "come as you are" format, responding to one major regional war and a series of crises around the world with equipment and doctrine optimized for that earlier Cold War era. In some sense, the momentum of the acquisition process is now resulting in a mismatch of capability with respect to emerging needs. Although one perception is that the Army now has more combat capability than it may need, which may result in inefficiencies, another perception is that the Army does not have the right kind of capability, which may result in an inability to operate effectively in future contingencies.

The fundamental strength of today's Army lies in its ability to fight and win a major theater-level war, and this ability exists through a deliberate intent to field the most capable mechanized force possible. It is easy to argue that the Army leadership succeeded in this intent, since no anticipated enemy force can match the firepower and maneuver capability of a combined arms mechanized U.S. force, equipped with the M1-series Abrams main battle tank, the M2-series Bradley infantry fighting vehicle, and the AH-64 Apache attack helicopter. Nonetheless, as the world continues to thaw out from the stability once imposed by a bipolar superpower rivalry, the likelihood of major theater-level war is giving way to increased numbers of smaller regional conflicts and crises. New crises and conflicts are continuing to emerge around the world, and as the frequency of such events continues to increase, so does the need to adjust the U.S. capability for direct response to, and intervention within, these situations.

Both the U.S. Army and U.S. Marine Corps have a capability for rapid reaction through their prepositioned forces. But these capabilities tend to be limited in application to a locality (in the case of land prepositioned forces) and littoral regions (in the case of afloat prepositioned forces). Through its *Global Engagement* vision, the U.S. Air Force has reshaped its overarching strategy for conventional rapid-reaction capability around the world, given that air power is inherently suited for such responsiveness. But as potent as modern air power has become, by itself it has proved inadequate for decisively resolving certain kinds of crises. Thus, there is a recognized need for ground forces that can go anywhere and respond rapidly. To address this need, both the Secretary of the Army and the Chief of Staff of the Army are calling for a fundamental change in strategy. More specifically, they are calling for developing forces that are *strategically responsive across the full spectrum of military operations*. Although there is new dialogue on what might be done, there is also considerable research that has examined many of the issues now coming to light, such as, "How might light forces be changed to offer greater rapid-reaction capability?"

This executive summary synthesizes research drawn from numerous studies conducted by the authors in the past few years on the topic of improving light air-deployable forces. The full report, MR-1196-A/OSD, provides more detail for the analysis and conclusions presented in this document. The focus is on the topic of new operational concepts along with the underlying enabling technologies. Three very different means for improving rapid-reaction capability are considered and analyzed in detail, with both strengths and weaknesses included in the assessment. The report was written primarily for the soldiers who will be developing such future capabilities; this executive summary was written primarily for policymakers and technologists involved in improving rapid-reaction capability.

Information used to support this executive summary was taken from research conducted by the authors for the following sponsors: the Defense Science Board (DSB) with GEN (ret.) David Maddox and Dr. Donald Latham; the Office of the Secretary of the Army for Research, Development, and Acquisition (SARDA) with Dr. A. Fenner Milton; the Defense Advanced Research Projects Agency (DARPA) with Dr. David Whelan; and U.S. Army Training and Doctrine Command (TRADOC) with MG Robert Scales, Jr. The research projects were conducted within the Force Development and Technology Program of RAND Arroyo Center and the Acquisition and Technology Policy Center of RAND's National Defense Research Institute (NDRI). Both the Arroyo Center and NDRI are federally funded research and development centers, the first one sponsored by the United States Army, the second one sponsored by the Office of the Secretary of Defense, the Joint Staff, the unified commands, and the defense agencies. Questions about this book can be forwarded to:

John Matsumura
1700 Main Street
Santa Monica, CA 90407
e-mail: John_Matsumura@rand.org

Contents

Figures

Tables

Abbreviations

AAA	Anti-aircraft artillery
AAA	Anti-aircraft artillery
ACTD	Advanced Concept Technology Demonstration
ADAS	Air-deliverable acoustic sensor
AGS	Armored gun system
APC	Armored personnel carrier
BDA	Battle damage assessment
C2	Command and control
CONUS	Continental United States
DARPA	Defense Advanced Research Projects Agency
DPICM	Dual-purpose improved conventional munition
DRB	Division Ready Brigade
DSB	Defense Science Board
EFOG-M	Enhanced fiber-optic guided missile
FLIR	Forward-looking infrared
GPS	Global positioning system
HE	High explosive
HIMARS	High-mobility artillery rocket system
HMMWV	High-mobility, multipurpose wheeled vehicle
IRC	Immediate ready company
JSOW	Joint Standoff Weapon
JTF	Joint Task Force
KEM	Kinetic-energy missile
LANTCOM	Latin America–Atlantic Command
LER	Loss-exchange ratio
LOS	Line of sight
LOSAT	Line-of-sight anti-tank
MANPADS	Man-portable air defense systems
MLRS	Multiple-launch rocket system
MOE	Measure of effectiveness
MOUT	Military operations on urban terrain
MRL	Multiple rocket launcher
MTW	Major theater war
PGMM	Precision-guided mortar munition
RFPI	Rapid Force Projection Initiative
RSTA	Reconnaissance, surveillance, and target acquisition
SADARM	Sense and destroy armor
SAM	Surface-to-air missile
SARDA	Secretary of the Army for Research, Development, and Acquisition

SEAD   Suppression of enemy air defenses
SPH   Self-propelled howitzer
SUO   Small unit operations
SWA   Southwest Asia
TACCP   Tactical command post
TACMS   Tactical Missile System
TOC   Tactical operations center
TOT   Time on target
TOW   Tube-launched, optically-tracked, wire-guided
TRADOC   U.S. Army Training and Doctrine Command
TTP   Tactics, techniques, and procedures
UAV   Unmanned aerial vehicle
WAM   Wide-area munition

Chapter One

Introduction

The Vulnerability of U.S. Rapid-Reaction Capability

WHEN KUWAIT FELL TO INVADING IRAQI TROOPS on August 2, 1990, and Iraqi forces
made several incursions into Saudi territory, military logic dictated that the
Iraqis would continue their successful offensive and seize Saudi Arabian air-
fields, ports, and oil fields. To counter the expected offensive, the United
States sent the 2nd Brigade, 82nd Airborne Division—the Army's Division
Ready Brigade (DRB)—to defend the port at Al Jubayl to prepare for the ar-
rival of U.S. Marines.

But the Iraqi offensive never happened, and the brigade accomplished its
mission by default. Taking nothing away from the light forces deployed, the sit-
uation in Southwest Asia in 1990 was clearly nowhere near as "stressing" as
it might have been, because Hussein's heavier forces did not behave as one
would expect and did not take advantage of their apparent overmatch. Had
they advanced into Saudi Arabia, would the light forces in place have been able
to delay their advance without suffering massive casualties? Moreover, if Hussein's heavier forces had themselves been more capable, would the brigade's
much smaller and lighter forces have been lethal and survivable enough to have
had a decisive impact on the battle?

The experience in Southwest Asia raised the issue of the vulnerability of
U.S. light forces in such rapid-reaction situations—an issue that is growing in
response to changes in both the nature and uncertainties of conflict. In terms of
the nature of conflict, the spectrum of operations has become much more var-
ied and extensive, and light forces are playing new roles in humanitarian operations (like Somalia) and in major theater wars (MTWs) (like the Gulf War), in
addition to their traditional roles in counterinsurgency and terrorist operations.
Beyond such changes in the nature of conflict, there is more uncertainty about
where such conflicts can occur. Now, the potential for conflict is global in nature, which means that it is much more difficult for military planners to rely on
traditional prepositioned forces as a hedge against conflict breaking out. As a
result, rapid-reaction capabilities have become more critical.

Under the circumstances described here, the prospect of using light forces,
particularly airborne forces—which are intended to be deployed rapidly to
trouble spots—against larger and heavier forces in the early phase of conflict
has become an accepted reality. If light forces are to be used in this role, they
will need to have much greater survivability and lethality. Numerous studies
since the Gulf War have raised the issue of "the shortfall in rapid-reaction

capability"; unfortunately, ten years later, the shortfall still exists, as the recent Kosovo crisis reveals. Although the delay in bringing ground forces into Kosovo could be directly attributed to political indecision, it is probable that the indecision was linked to the risk of bringing current forces into the theater.

Options for Resolving the Shortfall in Rapid-Reaction Forces

Although the shortfall in rapid-reaction capability is generally well recognized, the solution for responding to it can take a range of forms, including not only changes in operational concept and equipment (new technologies) but also changes in force organization and design. This executive summary describes how RAND analysts, drawing on research conducted over the past few years, have examined three different paths for improving rapid-reaction capability. The paths are illustrated conceptually in Figure 1.1. Each path—presented in terms of the burden required to deploy it—represents a very different means to get to a similar end: a force that offers more overall capability than the current light airborne forces but is still very quickly deployable.

The First (Middle) Path: Enhancing Current Light Forces

This path examines what might be considered an evolutionary change from current rapidly deployable forces, such as the DRB of the 82nd Airborne. Here, the force remains as a small, mostly self-contained unit with a force structure similar to the DRB, but it is given the capability to fight and survive in a mission that might otherwise require a larger, heavier force. This could be accomplished by introducing a modified operational concept (or concepts) and by incorporating many underlying, enabling technologies, which include advanced

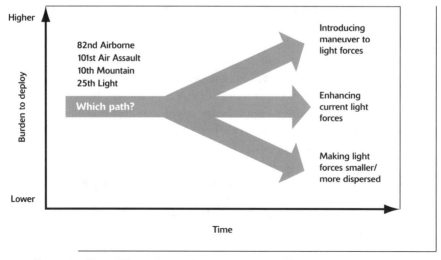

Figure 1.1—Three Different Paths to Developing a More Effective Rapid-Reaction Capability

reconnaissance, surveillance, and target acquisition (RSTA), command and control (C2), and weapon systems. These modified operational concepts involve substantially greater indirect-fire capability than what currently exists in a light force. More specifically, by linking precision munitions to a range of advanced indirect-fire weapons to an integrated sensor and C2 network, substantially more firepower can be brought to bear on an attacking enemy, essentially providing much greater indirect firepower and, thus, lethality at substantially longer ranges.

The Second (Lower) Path: Making Light Forces Smaller and More Dispersed

Another method for improving light forces involves altering the notion of area control by massed ground forces. Here, a very small, highly dispersed force would be deployed in a threatened region. These virtually independent dismounted teams would be equipped with advanced sensor systems for establishing on-site intelligence and would have advanced C2 to give them the capability to call in remotely located long-range fires. A very small and dispersed deploying force, it has been argued, would be difficult for the enemy to engage (e.g., presenting a spread-out target with no obvious center of mass); this force would thus be much more survivable than a typical rapid-reaction force. It was noted early on that such a force may not be capable of holding terrain, but might be sufficient for denying the enemy full use of it.

The Third (Upper) Path: Introducing Maneuver to Light Forces

Another method for responding to the limitations of current rapid-reaction capability is to make a major adjustment to the nature of the force itself. More specifically, new ideas and technologies are emerging that can enable some level of operational and tactical maneuver combined with rapid deployment. Vertical envelopment concepts being explored by the U.S. Army Training and Doctrine Command (TRADOC) are one example of such a major shift. Most of the rapid-reaction capability envisioned in these concepts are closer to heavy forces than to current-day light forces. That is, rather than emphasizing dismounted infantry, these concepts involve infantry mounted in lightweight but highly capable vehicles that could be airlifted close to battle positions by large inter/intratheater lifters or, possibly, by large rotary-wing, tilt-rotor, or tilt-wing aircraft.

Which Path to Choose? The Need for Sound Analysis

Ultimately, efforts to improve light forces to give them greater rapid-reaction capability, making them more lethal and survivable and more germane to future conflicts, require policymakers to make decisions now that will affect military capabilities down the road. These decisions—whether about organizational structure, force designs, new operational concepts, or enabling technologies—can lead to irrevocable consequences. Unfortunately, ideas that look good on paper do not always meet expectations when they are implemented. Thus, the answer to the question of what path or combination of paths to follow must be based on a sound analytic foundation that gives policymakers confidence in the choices they make.

The analyses summarized here are all driven by an extensive and broad-based simulation environment, which has evolved over many years of development at RAND. In an evolutionary manner, new concepts and technologies have been added into the simulation environment as needed to meet the objectives of the research. The process of developing the simulation environment has been an interactive one. In essence, building the environment (which included developing the scenarios used with it) involved importing and applying a wide range of analytic and simulation tools, refining the tools to represent new systems and technologies, and determining the appropriate level of model resolution. This resulted in the development of specialty models, such as acoustic models and smart-munition representations.

Using this simulation environment, RAND analysts evaluated each of the paths, starting first by laying out a base case against which to measure the paths—how the current light forces would have fared against a heavy force more competent than the one they faced in the Gulf War—and following the path analyses with an evaluation of some of the special challenges that go along with reshaping rapid-reaction forces for the future. Based on that evaluation, we find the following:

- In the base case, current-generation light forces do not fare well against a powerful, armored opponent.
- Making enhancements to the current-generation light forces (Path 1) strongly improves overall force effectiveness.
- Making light forces smaller/more dispersed (Path 2) has benefits but makes them more vulnerable and less capable.
- Introducing maneuver (Path 3) adds significant benefits, but the viability of creating such a force is unresolved.

Each of these findings is analyzed in more detail in the next four chapters. The final chapter raises some issues for policymakers in thinking about and implementing the paths.

Chapter Two

Current-Generation Light Forces Do Not Fare Well Against a Powerful, Armored Opponent

As we saw in Chapter One, when light forces were used in a rapid-reaction capacity to confront the heavier forces of Saddam Hussein's Army in Operation Desert Shield, they succeeded in their mission. However, as noted, they succeeded only by default, since the attack never came. In essence, the light forces performed as a deterrence force. But what if deterrence had failed and the attack *had* come—if Saddam's heavy forces had advanced and engaged the much lighter and less mobile American force that was screening the critical Saudi ports? Of course, that was August 1990. More than a decade later, how well would a light force equipped with modern capabilities fare in repelling a larger heavy force? When we conducted the analysis, the results were not encouraging. *Even with air and attack helicopter support, the current-generation light force proves to be at a significant disadvantage when confronting a capable heavy force.* Following a brief discussion of the context for the analysis, we discuss this finding in more detail.

Setting the Context for Analysis

To answer the question, analysts looked across three scenarios that vary across terrain type, threat, mission, and force mix, as summarized in Table 2.1. In essence, the first and second scenarios are the same except for the terrain. In the Southwest Asia (SWA) scenario (which is played out in Saudi Arabia), the terrain is open with long lines of sight (LOS), whereas in the East Europe scenario, the terrain is much closer. This variation enables analysts to explore the impact of terrain on force performance, particularly more stressing conditions (i.e., more limited LOS) and their influence on technology. Whereas in the first and second scenarios a full light infantry brigade (DRB) faces a heavy threat in a prepared defense, in the Latin America–Atlantic Command (LANTCOM) scenario a partially attrited DRB in the second phase of a forced-entry operation faces a slightly less heavy threat from a hasty defense.

As for the force mixes, the Blue forces shown for the first two scenarios are comparable to what the 82nd Airborne DRB consisted of in the Desert Storm time frame (around the time that the initial analysis was performed). Generally, this DRB has one airborne brigade headquarters company, three airborne infantry battalions, one artillery battalion (105mm towed), one air defense artillery battery, one attack helicopter company, one armor company, and one artillery battery (155mm towed). All told, the DRB includes 4,297 short tons of equipment and contains 3,450 soldiers. For the LANTCOM scenario, the Blue forces are similar (though attrited). Four armored gun system (AGS) platforms were included, since they were envisioned to be a key direct-fire system in the force. Although acquisition decisions have since eliminated this particular program, it was used here as a surrogate for a notional future direct-fire capability.

The Red forces possess some sophisticated weapons, including T-72S with AT-11 (fire-on-move) missiles, BMP-2 armored personnel carriers (APCs) with AT/P-6 missiles, self-propelled 120mm multiple rocket launchers (MRLs),

Table 2.1—Three Basic Scenarios and Key Distinguishing Parameters

Scenario	Terrain	Threat	Mission	Force Mix	
				Blue Forces	Red Forces
SWA	Open and flat, with moderate trafficability; LOS=3–5 km	Red heavy division consisting of two armor regiments attacking along two primary avenues of approach	Blue light infantry conducting prepared defense	15 HMMWV-Scouts 58 HMMWV-TOWs 54 Dragons 18 Stingers 6 Apaches 14 Sheridans 8 155mm howitzer 18 105mm howitzer	323 T-72S (Tanks) 219 BMP-2 (APCs) 35 RTR-60 (APCs) 30 120/180 MRL (rocket artillery) 72 152 SPH (cannon artillery) 16 HAVOC/HIND (helos)
East Europe	Close and rough, with limited trafficability; LOS=1–3 km	Same as above	Same as above	Same as above	Same as above
LANTCOM	Close and rolling hills (partially covered), with limited trafficability; LOS=1–5 km	Red heavy division (-) consisting of two brigades and a battalion attacking along three primary avenues of approach	Partially attrited Blue light infantry conducting hasty defense following a forced entry	34 HMMWV-TOWs 4 AGS 24 Javelin 6 Apaches 8 155mm howitzer 18 105mm howitzer	131 T-72S 131 BMP-2 6 120/180 MRL 12 152 SPH 6 HAVOC/HIND

and 152mm (2S3) howitzers, which are considered to be medium-to-hard targets, and mobile air defense units (2S6) with radar track 30mm guns and SA-19 missiles. The enemy does not have sophisticated overhead RSTA and must rely on command vehicle forward-looking infrared (FLIR) and visual recognition for the direct-fire engagement.

With this context, we now turn to discussing the main finding presented above.

Light Forces Lose, Driven Mostly by an Inefficient Indirect-Fire Battle

That the light forces do not fare very well is not surprising, given that the light forces are significantly outnumbered in the scenarios; the more interesting question is determining why the result occurs, something the analysis helps to uncover.

Figure 2.1 shows the timelines of the simulated battles for the three scenarios, broken up into two "spaces"—the indirect-fire and direct-fire battles.

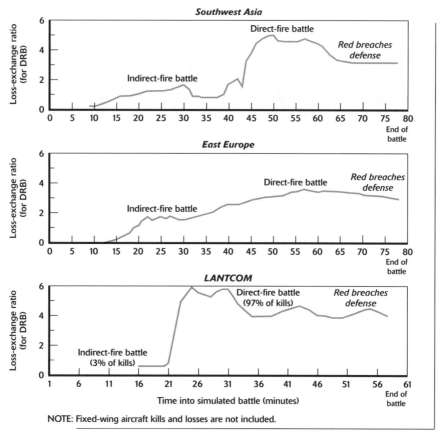

NOTE: Fixed-wing aircraft kills and losses are not included.

Figure 2.1—In All Three Scenarios, the DRB Loses the Battle

The pattern across all three scenarios is the same: The current-generation light force is unable to inflict enough damage on the advancing enemy armor with today's indirect-fire weapons, thus leading to an intense direct-fire engagement.

The timeline plots the DRB's loss-exchange ratio (LER)—the chosen outcome measure here—over the course of the simulated battle. The LER captures the ratio of Red system losses to Blue system losses. It is important to remember that in all scenarios, Red forces significantly outnumber Blue forces; thus, low ratios (even though positive for Blue forces) still result in poor overall battle outcomes. In general, the lower the ratio, the worse the outcome. In other words, LERs below about 5:1 or 6:1 usually mean that the Blue force loses the battle, while LERs up around 9:1 usually signify a draw and those above 10:1 usually constitute a win—i.e., Red is defeated in place and Blue has sufficient systems to continue to fight another engagement.

In examining the indirect-fire battle, we find that the current artillery systems, towed 105mm and 155mm howitzers (cannons) and the associated rounds (dual-purpose improved conventional munition (DPICM) and high explosive (HE)) do not provide significant attrition against the armored, mobile Red force—e.g., less than 3 percent of the attrition in the LANTCOM scenario. In the direct-fire (close) battle, the DRB's direct-fire weapons—led by the HMMWV-TOWs and the Sheridans and supported by the Apaches—outperformed those of the attacking force. With longer-range sensors and weapons reach, the DRB was generally able to start the close fight before the attacking force. This advantage, however, was short-lived. As the Red force continued its advance, the DRB range and reach advantage was reduced, resulting in a notable reduction to the overall LER—ultimately, between 3:1 and 5:1, depending on the scenario.

Direct-Fire Systems Are Vulnerable

The current-generation direct-fire systems are also very vulnerable. At the end of the close battle, the Blue forces had relatively few direct-fire systems intact. For example, of the original 58 HMMWV-TOWs in place at the start of the battle, only about 25 percent (15 weapons) remained at the end in the SWA scenario, and fewer remained in the East Europe scenario; the results were even worse for the 14 Sheridans, with only two remaining in SWA and one in East Europe. The main problem is that the two systems are forced to engage the enemy at points on the battlefield where they are exposed (within the LOS of the missiles and main guns of enemy systems).

The Results Across Scenarios Vary by Terrain Type

While the patterns of the results across the scenarios were all fairly similar, the results themselves did vary by terrain type. As shown in Table 2.1, the three scenarios were chosen to examine the impact of terrain type on DRB systems, varying from fairly flat terrain in SWA with long LOS to the close and rough terrain of East Europe, with much smaller LOS. Interestingly, the DRB did relatively better in the open terrain of SWA, where its TOWs could exploit their long range, whereas in the closer terrain of Eastern Europe and LANTCOM, the outcomes were worse, since the enemy could close the range into a more advantageous direct-fire battle. In addition, the terrain in East Europe precluded a successful Apache standoff attack.

Chapter Three

Making Enhancements to the Current-Generation Light Forces Strongly Improves Overall Force Effectiveness

IN CHAPTER ONE WE ARGUED THAT THERE WAS A SHORTFALL in the current capability of the light forces to repel a heavy force, while the analysis described in Chapter Two made that shortfall concrete: A light force such as the 82nd DRB equipped with modern capabilities—sensors, weapons, and support—does not fare well in a rapid-reaction role against a powerful, armored opponent. Given this outcome, what possible solutions might be available in the near future to enhance the current light forces and improve this outcome? When we analytically examined enhancements needed to do this, we found that without changing numbers of systems, required lift, organization, or mission, *new systems and tactics could strongly improve overall force effectiveness.* Following a brief discussion of the context for the analysis, we explore this finding in more detail.

Setting the Context for Analysis

To determine what near-term solution might be possible, analysts examined the results of upgrading current rapid-reaction forces—as presented in the base case established in Chapter Two—with a near-term concept and with enabling technologies, focusing on some combination of systems similar to those experimented with in the Rapid Force Projection Initiative (RFPI) Advanced Concept Technology Demonstration (ACTD), whose goal was to "put maturing technologies in the hands of soldiers" to allow them to evaluate the utility of technologies firsthand.

Taking light forces down this path would keep the structure of today's light forces basically intact, but it would increase survivability and lethality by adding some improved direct-fire systems and by employing a hunter–standoff killer concept as the indirect-fire system. The hunter–standoff killer enables the light force to engage an attacking enemy from much farther out, allowing the force to capitalize on already-proven advanced technologies. Figure 3.1 illustrates the concept.

Hunters—manned and unmanned, air or ground, and mobile or stationary—sense the presence, position, and status of enemy systems. They communicate the intelligence and targeting data to C2 nodes, which quickly match

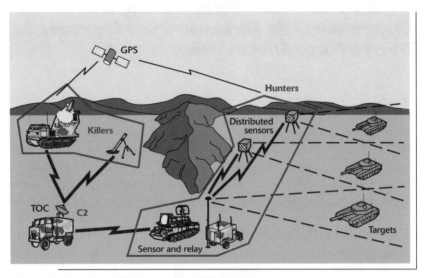

Figure 3.1—Depiction of the Hunter–Standoff Killer Concept

targets to weapons based on range, availability, and effectiveness. Killers—ranging from mortars to cannons to missiles—fire different types of munitions at the targets. Battle damage assessment may sometimes be done by the hunters and possibly the weapons themselves. Global positioning system (GPS) technology can be used extensively throughout the force for positioning and navigation.

Table 3.1 shows how the force mix was adjusted for the three scenarios to create the "enhanced DRB," with entries in boldface reflecting changes to the base case force mixes shown in Table 2.1. Direct-fire capability was improved by substituting out Dragons and Sheridans for Javelins and AGS, respectively, systems that the U.S. Army was pursuing at the time of the analysis. The indirect-fire hunter–standoff killer capability was represented by a reduced-signature hunter vehicle (with mast-mounted sensors) and the enhanced fiber-optic guided missile (EFOG-M). As shown in Figure 3.1, the two systems work as a team, with the forward-positioned hunter vehicle acquiring the target and handing it off to the more safely positioned EFOG-M platform. Finally, "fast C2" was added to the hunter–standoff killer based on the Army light tactical operations center (TOC). In adjusting the force mix, airlift was assumed to be fixed; given this constraint, the direct-fire systems—the Dragons/Sheridans to Javelins/AGS—were one-to-one substitutions, while the indirect-fire systems were swapped out at a precalculated weight ratio, reflected in the numbers shown in the table.

With this context, we now turn to discussing the main finding presented above.

Table 3.1—Base Case and Improved DRB Force Mix for the Three Scenarios

Scenarios	Blue Forces: Base Case DRB	Blue Forces: Upgraded DRB	Red Forces
SWA	15 HMMWV-Scouts 54 Dragons 18 Stingers 6 Apaches 14 Sheridans 8 M198s 58 HMMWV-TOWs	15 HMMWV-Scouts 54 Javelin 18 Stingers 6 Apaches 14 AGS 18 HMMWV-TOWs 24 Hunter 18 EFOG-M	323 T-72S (Tanks) 219 BMP-2 (APCs) 35 RTR-60 (APCs) 30 120/180 MRL (rocket artillery) 72 152 SPH (cannon artillery) 16 HAVOC/HIND (helicopters)
East Europe	Same as above	Same as above	Same as above
LANTCOM	34 HMMWV-TOWs 4 AGS 24 Javelin 6 Apaches 8 155mm howitzer 18 105mm howitzer 18 Forward Observers 2 UAV	13 HMMWV-TOWs 4 AGS[a] 24 Javelin 6 Apaches 8 155mm howitzer 18 105mm howitzer 12 EFOG-M 18 Forward Observers 2 UAV 6 Hunter 18 Remote Sentry 36 Overwatch Sensors	131 T-72S 131 BMP-2 6 120/180 MRL 12 152 SPH 6 HAVOC/HIND

a At the time the analysis was conducted, systems like the Sheridan were still integral to the 82nd Airborne's DRB. In addition, the Army was considering introducing the AGS as a replacement for the Sheridan, plus elsewhere in the force structure.

Light Forces Are More Successful, Driven Mostly by the Hunter–Standoff Killer Capability

Replacing direct- and indirect-fire systems, adding air and ground sensors, and streamlining the C2 system allowed the force to operate successfully, even though it was outnumbered by attacking enemy armor. Figure 3.2 presents an updated version of Figure 2.1, showing the base case performance of the DRB in relation to the enhanced DRB. While in the baseline DRB the LER was not good enough to successfully defend against the Red force, the enhanced DRB decisively stopped the attack in the SWA scenario and marginally fought to a draw in the tougher terrain of the East Europe and LANTCOM scenarios. In the SWA scenario, in particular, the LER was (as the figure shows) actually as high as 30 at the end of the indirect-fire battle. The contribution of the

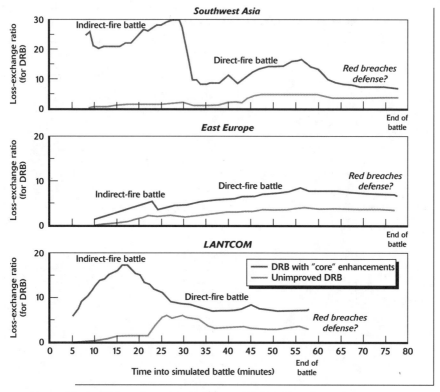

Figure 3.2—In All Three Scenarios, the Enhanced DRB Is More Successful

hunter–standoff killer systems in this scenario is very evident—the battle could start much sooner and could be waged at much longer ranges, well before the main force became susceptible to Red's direct-fire assets. Although not as dramatic, the impact of the hunter–standoff killer systems in the East Europe scenario is still quite evident. The LER improved by a factor of two leading into the direct-fire battle. In the LANTCOM scenario (here with EFOG-M placed forward), Blue begins with a high LER because of EFOG-M kills. The upgraded DRB then moves into the direct-fire phase with a much more favorable force ratio than was present with the baseline DRB.

Of the various weapons in the enhanced DRB, EFOG-M was the most efficient, especially in the SWA and LANTCOM scenarios, where the system contributed 48 and 53 percent of the kills, respectively. The substitution of the Javelin for the Dragon system in the direct-fire battle also provided a higher share of the overall force lethality, especially in the East Europe case, where it was responsible for nearly 40 percent of the kills.

Defending Against an Advanced Threat Requires a Richer Mix of Sensors and Weapon Systems

While the enhanced DRB does much better against a current threat, how would it fare against a more sophisticated future enemy threat—one with better sensors (FLIRs), armor (state-of-the-art Russian tanks and armored personnel carriers), weapons (longer-range and smarter munitions), and air defenses (high-end SA-15s and SA-19s)? Not surprisingly, the performance of the enhanced DRB is significantly reduced by all the additions.

To counter the improved threat, we enhanced the DRB again with additional RFPI systems: two RSTA systems—remote sentry (FLIR with acoustic cuer), and an unmanned aerial vehicle (UAV); a direct-fire system—line-of-sight anti-tank (LOSAT), which is a kinetic-energy missile (KEM) that can be fired from pods; and two other indirect-fire systems—precision-guided mortar munitions (PGMM), and the high-mobility artillery rocket system (HIMARS) with a pod of multiple-launch rocket systems (MLRS) containing sense and destroy armor (SADARM). Finally, we added in an obstacle system, the wide-area munition (WAM), and an autonomous vehicle capable of engaging combat vehicles out to a 100-meter range.

Figure 3.3 shows the impact of each RFPI system on the upgraded DRB LER. We found that most systems can provide at least some further improvement to the LER, but these tend to be relatively incremental improvements at best. The UAV did not survive in East Europe against radar-guided air defenses. The short-range PGMMs were competing with the direct-fire systems and consequently did not provide meaningful improvement to the LER. HIMARS as an individual system traded in to the DRB was seen to be effective in SWA, but it was not assessed in East Europe because there were not enough sightings

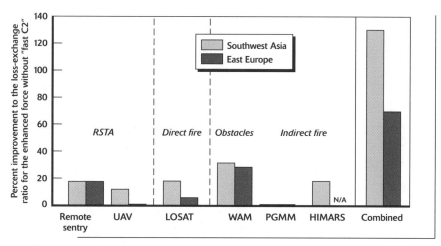

Figure 3.3—Effect of Additional DRB Upgrades on LERs in Southwest Asia and East Europe Scenarios

of company-sized targets by the hunter sensors to call for this type of massed fire. Interestingly enough, when all the listed systems are included in the simulation (the combined bars in the figure), there was a complementary improvement to the overall LER. One example of this: WAM slows down the Red force and presents more opportunities for the other Blue indirect-fire weapons to engage the force from afar. The end result is improvements around 140 percent in the SWA scenario and around 80 percent in Eastern Europe.

With the improvements from the combined case, the DRB easily wins the battle in SWA but struggles barely to a draw in East Europe, in part because the relatively small-footprint smart munitions that were added were unable to effectively "encounter" mobile targets in a dispersed attack formation and in part because the forward-positioned sensors (manned hunter vehicles, remote sentries, and UAVs) did not survive throughout the engagement in East Europe.

To counter these problems, we added in a larger-footprint submunition (3x radius) to increase the probability of "encounter" and a large (300-element) sensor called the air-deliverable acoustic sensor (ADAS). With these additions, the DRB was able to improve the LER to the point where a decisive win was attained. As it turns out, the more advanced artillery with a larger-footprint smart munition was not sufficient to provide a win. Rather, the lack of a good RSTA system proved to be the deciding factor.

Chapter Four

Making Light Forces Smaller/More Dispersible Has Benefits But Makes Them More Vulnerable and Less Capable

IN CHAPTER THREE WE EXAMINED some relatively near-term upgrades to improve the capability of light forces when placed in rapid-reaction missions, working mostly with RFPI concepts and technologies within the context of ACTDs. But what would be the impact of changing concepts—for example, making light forces smaller and more dispersed? Given that the dramatic improvements in precision-guided and smart weapons can enable a greater share of battlefield firepower to be brought in from great distances (as shown in the last chapter), a smaller presence of organic weapons would theoretically be possible, which means the ground force itself can be made smaller. By making the ground force smaller and lighter, many units could be placed on a battlefield fairly quickly, even faster than a traditional light airborne unit; by also dispersing it, the force would be a much more difficult target for enemy forces. In fact, when we do the analysis, we find that *there was considerable merit in making light forces even smaller than they are now, particularly in that they can deploy with greater speed; however, there were major vulnerabilities and limitations in the kinds of missions that such forces could accomplish.* Following a brief discussion of the context for the analysis, we discuss this finding in more detail.

Setting the Context for Analysis

Here, we analyze three recent initiatives that have examined the idea of making light forces smaller and more capable. The first, based on a Defense Science Board (DSB) concept, is a small, mostly self-contained unit, such as a DRB, that is given the mission and capability of a larger unit, such as a division, by augmenting many of the DRB's current components with advanced RSTA, C2, and weapon systems and removing less relevant systems. While similar in some ways to the RFPI ACTD, this concept, rather than emphasizing organic capability, relies on joint "external" capabilities, such as remotely located RSTA and long-range fire-support system technologies.

The second initiative, based on the TRADOC light battle force concept, is like the DSB concept in that it also relies extensively on both high levels of RSTA and remote, long-range weapons, referred to here as "reachback" weapons. However, it goes further by making the unit completely dispersed, no longer occupying a specific area, and by replacing the weapon systems with immobile weapon "pods" that can house a wide range of precision-guided weapons.

The third initiative, based on the Defense Advanced Research Projects Agency (DARPA) small unit operations (SUO) concept, has three echelons: small (7- to 9-man) teams with some local fire support, a tactical command post (TACCP) able to call in fires from the short- and mid-range organic assets, and a Joint Task Force (JTF) able to direct fires from long-range standoff weapons. The force has many nonmobile, unmanned assets dispersed through the region to help it accomplish its mission, including detection and targeting sensors, communication relays, and short- and long-range missile pods, similar to those in the TRADOC concept.

With this context, we now turn to discussing the main finding presented above.

Making Light Forces Smaller Makes Them More Deployable . . .

All three concepts are different, but they have one thing in common: They are, by definition, much smaller than the DRB they are replacing and, thus, more deployable. For example, the SUO force is substantially smaller than the 82nd DRB—less than one-fourth the size (1,600 short tons versus 7,100 short tons, including combat support), even assuming pessimistic assumptions on the number of personnel (400) and heavy expenditures of missiles and pods. In fact, the use of containerized missiles in place of vehicles may make the force more efficient to transport. The time needed to move to East Europe, for example, under the assumption of 40 percent airlift availability drops from five days (for the 82nd DRB) to less than two days.

. . . While Greater Dispersion Makes Them Somewhat More Survivable

Dispersion is also a part of all three concepts and also shows promise. In the DSB concept, for example, the light forces were dispersed so that the force expanded by 5–6 times compared to the original formation for the 82nd DRB. Despite the dispersion, interlocking, supporting fires were still possible between the battalions, and overall Blue losses to Red artillery were reduced in the indirect-fire battle. However, survivability did suffer more in the direct-fire battle because the larger perimeter resulted in less efficient overlapping fields of acquisition and fire for Blue and permitted more efficient simultaneous application of Red firepower.

However, the Smaller Light Forces Are More Vulnerable

The latter result above calls attention to one area of vulnerability for the smaller light forces. All three concepts are based on the assumption that the direct-fire battle will be minimized by the use of precision nonorganic reach-

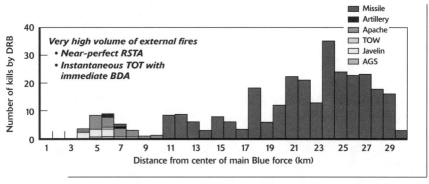

Figure 4.1—Effect of Relying on Reachback Weapon Systems in Best Case Scenario

back weapon systems and a limited number of organic indirect-fire systems. The lighter forces are lighter in part because they are less armored and protected, relying on dispersion and signature reduction for protection. However, in all the concepts simulated, there is still a direct-fire battle. For example, in the DSB concept, which relies primarily on enhanced external RSTA systems and nonorganic reachback systems, the analysis shows (Figure 4.1) that even when we assume near-perfect intelligence, an instantaneous time on target (TOT) with immediate battle damage assessment (BDA) for the large-footprint reachback weapons, and a very high volume of fires (roughly four times what was projected for the base case), a significant portion of the attacking enemy force survives to fight the direct-fire battle. Ultimately, 306 of the 695 Red systems are destroyed, with 279 of those systems destroyed by the reachback weapon systems 11 kilometers and back from the center of the main Blue force.

The TRADOC concept—with its reliance on reachback weapons and immobile indirect-fire pods—reveals a similar vulnerability. While the analysis showed the use of the two systems was quite effective in attriting the enemy force, the success comes at a cost. If the battle continues until the end—150 minutes—over a third of the battle unit can be lost to enemy fires, mostly resulting from receiving direct fire from the surviving enemy air and ground units.

Another vulnerability of all the concepts is that they rely on complicated RSTA systems to compensate for the dispersion of the forces, and these systems must operate effectively for the concepts to succeed. For example, the DRB concept relies on many steps to operate effectively—acquiring targets, passing information, assigning weapons, dispensing munitions, performing battle damage assessment, and many others. Similarly, the SUO concept requires comprehensively sensing all relevant information—enemy position, composition, and status; own locations; terrain and weather; etc.—being able to communicate and display this information quickly and accurately to all sites that need it, and then using precision standoff weapons to defeat the targets located. One of the more vulnerable areas for the SUO force is that there are many stages of coordination required to successfully target mid- to long-range precision indirect fires. All these new capabilities will require new tactics, techniques, and procedures (TTPs), and some of them may open up opportunities for the enemy.

Beyond these two vulnerabilities, the concepts all require forces with limited maneuverability. For example, the TRADOC light battle units were limited by their lack of maneuver capability. In several instances, they were not able to reposition out of harm's way from the large attacking force. Also, they were unable to exploit the effects of the simultaneous and highly effective indirect-fire attacks, which, in theory, could have led to greater overall force synergy.

And the Smaller Light Forces Are Also More Mission-Limited

While the forces in the three concepts are vulnerable, they are also more limited in the kinds of missions they could accomplish. For example, a small dispersed force would likely have to rely more on remotely located, reachback weapons for its lethality. As a result, instead of holding terrain as a typical light airborne force may be required to do, the best this force might expect to accomplish with such weapons would be to deny the enemy use of terrain.

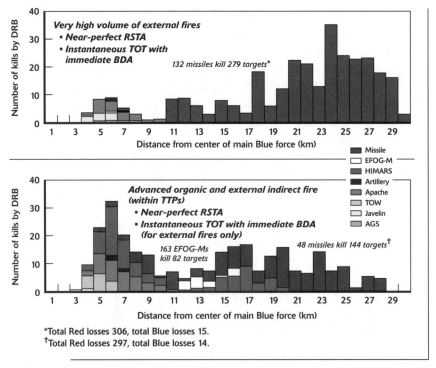

*Total Red losses 306, total Blue losses 15.
†Total Red losses 297, total Blue losses 14.

Figure 4.2—Effect of a More Balanced Mix Between Organic and External Fires

Given this, a force equipped with organic firepower appears to be essential, especially so when either an objective must be protected or an area denied to the enemy.

Although our research does suggest that the amount of organic capability can be reduced given a significant presence of effective external RSTA and fire support, the most attractive and robust solution for enhancing the capability of small forces is a mix between advanced organic systems and external systems, as shown in Figure 4.2. The top part of the figure reproduces the chart shown in Figure 4.1—the very high volume missile attack—and results in large numbers of kills at deep ranges, but the ability to attrit (and level of efficiency) drops off at closer ranges—resulting in a small residual direct-fire battle. In contrast, the more balanced attack, which uses standard TTPs, results in relatively moderate attrition at deep ranges, and many of the closer-in engagements are handled by more efficient organic indirect fires. High-value enemy artillery targets are targeted primarily by HIMARS/Damocles, while armor is primarily targeted by EFOG-M. The "shape" of the attrition is significantly different between the long-range external and combined external/organic cases, but the outcomes, in terms of direct-fire battle intensity and overall LER, are quite similar.

Unfortunately, equipping such a force with significant organic firepower effectively makes it less of a "small" force, increasing both its signature and its deployment time.

Chapter Five

Introducing Maneuver Adds Significant Benefits, But the Viability of Creating and Deploying Such a Force Is Unresolved

IN CHAPTER FOUR WE EXPLORED A CHANGE from conventional light forces by making them smaller and more dispersed (the path 2 option). One of the key limitations of the reconfigured light forces was that they were more vulnerable than conventional light forces, both because they were lighter and because they were limited in their ability to maneuver on the battlefield. In some cases, the use of precision remote fires was able to open up opportunities that the smaller, more dispersed forces were unable to exploit because they could not maneuver to do so. In this chapter we examine changes in the other direction: the path 3 option, which introduced maneuver—combined operational and tactical—to light forces, thus giving them more capability than they currently have but also making them heavier than they are now. *When we conduct the analysis, we find that introducing maneuver capabilities yields significant benefits but requires significant and fundamental changes for the concept to be viable.* Following a brief discussion of the context for the analysis, we discuss this finding in more detail.

Setting the Context for Analysis

Unlike the previous concepts examined, which involved emplacing a relatively stationary ground force that relied heavily on remote fires for survivability and lethality, the concept examined here concentrates on adding combined tactical and operational maneuver by introducing a light- to medium-weight family of vehicles within a force to accomplish rapid-reaction mission objectives. Although streamlined CONUS-to-battlefield positions are assumed in the concept, two major phases were considered: (1) an air insertion of the force, and (2) the ground combat itself. Both phases must be successfully completed for overall mission success.[1] In the air-insertion phase, we examined the capability of a notional advanced airframe—an air transport with a relatively large fuselage that employed tilt-rotor technology (roughly a C-130-sized aircraft)—to insert a ground force into the enemy rear area under different assumptions and conditions. For the ground-combat phase, we examined three different operational concepts with differing levels of ground maneuver. In all cases, this involved an early-entry neutralization or disruption of a mobile, elite

---

1 The air insertion phase is treated here with much more attention because a mounted force will likely require much greater "access" to the airspace than a dismounted infantry-based force assessed in the previous chapters.

enemy unit located behind enemy lines, and all concepts aggressively used long-range attack weapons, such as aircraft delivering standoff weapons like Joint Standoff Weapon (JSOW) and ballistic missiles like Navy and Army versions of the Tactical Missile System (TACMS).

However, the three concepts were quite distinct in the level of tactical maneuver and in subsequent application of force. The first concept concentrated solely on standoff attack, using B-2 and F-15 delivered JSOW and Navy and Army versions of TACMS cued by observers on the ground. These long-range weapons attempt to stop the advance of the elite enemy units. The second concept involved inserting a consolidated force (an advanced infantry battalion with two IRCs, or immediate ready companies) in addition to the standoff fires. The third concept changes the picture to one of dispersed U.S. forces inserted deep to disrupt and attrit the enemy force throughout the battlespace. This concept was developed by the Office of the Secretary of the Army for Research, Development, and Acquisition (SARDA) but is also shared by TRADOC through its Army After Next and Mobile Strike Force research. This particular application employed a small ten-team force using three of the seven types of vehicles specified in the SARDA concept—a family of tracked and wheeled vehicles of roughly 20 tons that are airliftable on C-130s.

Given the two phases, both air defense and ground force threats were modeled. The air-defense threat was a sophisticated integrated air defense network, intended to represent a "high end" opponent of the 2020 era. This included long-range, high-end systems, such as Russian SA-12s and SA-17s, emplaced throughout the depth of the battlespace. Since these are relatively mobile, tactical surface-to-air missiles (SAMs), they can accompany the advancing mechanized formation. The threat also included medium-range systems, such as SA-15s, and short-range systems, such as 2S6s, SA-18 man-portable air defense systems (MANPADS), and anti-aircraft artillery (AAA) in the network. To make the threat more formidable, the air-defense system was "partially integrated" in the simulation, as opposed to operating in stand-alone mode.

This ground force threat, consisting of the lead regiment of a division en route to the front, is intended to represent a high-quality threat of the 2020–2025 period. It includes a mix of sophisticated ground vehicles (direct and indirect fire), plus supporting attack helicopters from its parent division. The regiment also includes powerful air defenses in the form of 2S6 and SA-15 self-propelled systems. Some of these air defenses may have been attached from division level. All told, it includes 550 enemy systems.

With this context, we now turn to discussing the main finding presented above.

Of the Three Concepts, the Third One—Relying on Agile Maneuver—Is Most Effective

Figure 5.1 summarizes the effectiveness of the three ground force maneuver concepts in terms of a different set of measures of effectiveness than we have used previously. While we do represent enemy attrition (and own losses), shown on the "level of destruction" axis and in the numbers next to each concept, the dynamics of the ground battle in this analysis are such that disruption of the enemy operation—denying him the ability to move or resupply, slowing his progress, dispersing his forces, or degrading his coordination capabilities—may be as important as attrition. Shock effects (heavy losses over short time, in small areas, or of key systems) may also disrupt the advance. This measure of effectiveness is represented by the "degree of disruption" axis. As shown by the curve in Figure 5.1, some combination of these two factors should be sufficient to change enemy behavior.

As shown, concept 1—standoff attack alone—achieved a limited amount of attrition (killing a maximum of 79 of the 550 enemy systems in the lead regiment), although there were no losses, since direct exposure to the enemy was minimal. If foliage was omitted (e.g., in a separate "bald earth" run), 195 kills were obtained. However, enemy countermeasures such as the use of decoys, active protection systems, and force dispersion could reduce the kills below that achieved earlier. In all these cases, the enemy might suffer little disruption. The standoff strikes seldom hit specific, high-value vehicles, such as C2 or bridging assets, and do not have a localized "shock" effect. Rather, they attrit sporadically along the column, and the hulks would be expected to provide little obstacle to movement, particularly in this trafficable terrain. Only in the case with no cover would significant disruption be expected. These results sug-

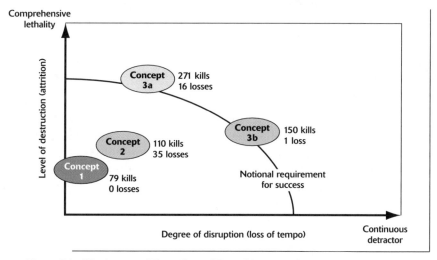

Figure 5.1—Effectiveness of Three Ground Force Maneuver Concepts

gest that firepower alone, operating in the absence of friendly maneuver units, would be limited in its ability to stop a rapidly advancing enemy force.

In concept 2—standoff munitions plus ground force maneuver—the lethality of the U.S. response increases, as does the force's robustness, where weapons in close proximity (e.g., direct fire) can be significantly more difficult to countermeasure. Nonetheless, since this force, once in place, lacks mobility on a par with the enemy, it can be bypassed. Even if the enemy chooses to engage this force, depending on the circumstances, it can opt to either fight with its overwhelming numbers or break off a smaller unit to contain this force. The lack of tactical mobility of this U.S. force is significant.

Concept 3a—standoff munitions with agile maneuver—achieved sufficient lethality to probably stop the Red force, even if disruption were not considered. Disruption was also present because of the shock associated with the ambush,[2] because of the ability of the direct-fire and organic indirect-fire systems to target specific high-value targets, and because of the presence of a capable force threatening the enemy rear, which may compel the opponent to change his plans. Red countermeasures are likely to reduce the impact of this force, but the effects should be limited because there are many different targeting mechanisms in concept 3a, including long- and short-timeline systems, autonomous and man-in-the-loop control, seekers using different spectra, and direct-fire systems able to sweep the battlefield.

Concept 3b represents a variant of 3a, using standoff munitions with agile maneuver against "soft" (e.g., resupply vehicles)—as opposed to "hard" (e.g., tanks)—targets. Since the agile ground forces were competing with long-range standoff fires for the same more lucrative logistics and supply vehicles (combat support targets), overall lethality was not as high as in 3b. However, because there was considerably more focused lethality on a specific target set, where all the additional kills were directed against the soft logistics and supply vehicles, the effect of disruption would be significantly, perhaps exponentially, higher. How much higher remains to be quantified.

However, the Viability of Creating—and Deploying—Such a Force Is Unresolved

While the positive outcomes seen with agile maneuver will not represent a major surprise to the ground warfighting community at large, the *viability* of creating and deploying such a force capability still remains to be resolved. Obvious challenges that still remain for enabling the vertical envelopment concepts include the technological feasibility of creating relatively lightweight, lethal, and survivable ground vehicles, the ability to support and resupply the ground

---

2 Once the local ambush began, a large proportion of the kills were achieved within a relatively short time, roughly five minutes.

force, and the ability to operationally deploy such a force without unacceptable losses to enemy air defenses. In terms of creating such a force, not only would it involve a complete reequipping of at least a portion of today's ground forces, it would also entail a reorganization of how such a force would need to fight, including training and doctrine changes.

As for deploying such a force, this was explicitly modeled in the analysis, which looked at the survivability of advanced air transports flying at different altitudes and speeds (e.g., low and slow, low and fast, and mid-altitude); with different levels of situational awareness (e.g., no SEAD (suppression of enemy air defenses), medium SEAD, and high SEAD); and with different levels of stealthiness (e.g., base case signature and low-observable signature). The result is a fairly daunting challenge:

- With low-altitude ingress and some situational awareness of emitter locations, the aircraft can avoid SA-12s, and some SA-15s, SA-17s, and 2S6s, but not all radio frequency SAM systems could be avoided.
- High levels of SEAD will be needed to countermeasure emitting air defense systems. Even one long-range radio frequency SAM site can inflict significant damage to the squadron.
- Stealth and large amounts of responsive SEAD are required to counter the effectiveness of AAA and MANPADs during low-altitude ingress.
- Mid-altitude ingress (above 15,000 feet) is a viable option if the long-range SAMs can be suppressed and the landing area secured from AAA and MANPADs.

While new technologies offer some promise in overcoming creation and deployment challenges, it is still too early to determine definitively how applicable many will be. As more research and experiments are conducted, better assessments on both the viability and the utility of maneuver for rapid-reaction missions can be made.

Chapter Six

How Can the Army Improve Rapid-Reaction Capability?

IN CHAPTER TWO WE SHOWED THAT CURRENT LIGHT FORCES have inadequate fire-power, mobility, and protection for many missions, particularly for missions that pit such forces against larger and heavier enemy forces. Given that finding, the subsequent three chapters addressed three different paths for remedying that shortfall. Each of those sections presented the paths and their analytic underpinnings, highlighting their strengths and weaknesses in isolation. In this chapter we step back and take a broader perspective, first comparing across the three paths and then presenting a strategy for improving rapid-reaction capability.

Comparing Across the Three Paths: Force Applicability and Implementability

One way to evaluate the three paths is to assess them in terms of a framework that measures the light forces they create against a number of critical mission parameters. On the surface, given all the changes occurring in the geopolitical arena, basic planning suggests that the Army should reshape light forces along the following parameters:

- The kind of missions it will need to address (e.g., peace operations, forced entry, area defense, local attack).
- The environment that it will need to operate in (e.g., open, closed, urban, contaminated).
- The level of threat it will need to defeat (e.g., size, level of sophistication).
- The kind or nature of threat it will have to address (e.g., militia, light infantry, mechanized, combined arms).
- The responsiveness with which it will need to deploy (e.g., few days, week, few weeks).

Although each parameter represents a significant challenge by itself, the parameters are often interwoven. In some sense, while the overall magnitude of the threat may have been decreasing, the number and complexity of threats has been on the rise. This uncertainty has compounded the rapid-reaction challenge.

Table 6.1 summarizes our assessment of the three paths in terms of whether the light forces created have more, less, or about the same capability

Table 6.1—Relative Impact of Paths for Improving Capability of Light Forces
(Over Current Light Forces)

Critical Rapid-Reaction Parameters	Path 1: Enhance Current Light Forces	Path 2: Make Light Forces Smaller and More Dispersed	Path 3: Introduce Maneuver to Light Forces
Kind of Mission	No change	Decrease	Significant increase
Type of Environment	No change	No change	Increase or decrease
Level of Threat	Increase	No change	Significant increase
Kind of Threat	Increase	Decrease	Significant increase
Responsiveness into Theater	No change	Significant increase	Decrease

as the current light force. On the whole, while all three paths offer significant benefits over a current light force, they also come with some drawbacks in relation to these five parameters.

Kind of mission. By adding maneuver, path 3 addresses head-on the fundamental issue of the "globalization" of threats. Although path 2 is revolutionary in form, it would result in a decrease in mission robustness over current light airborne forces. In particular, it might require sacrificing mission objectives to minimize casualties, and the path 2 force might have difficulty holding terrain—an element that may be of greater, not less, importance in the future.

Type of environment. All three paths offered only marginal improvements in the emerging environments that U.S. forces will face—complex terrain, low-intensity conflict, etc. The only exception was path 3, which could improve force applicability in military operations on urban terrain (MOUT) or in a contaminated environment, owing to the added protection of advanced, highly mobile vehicles. However, the same vehicles could well be ineffective in constrictive terrain, such as jungle environments, where dismounted infantry aided by dispersed sensors and relatively short-range, personal weapons might be the primary option.

Level and kind of threat. Both path 1 and path 3 provided improvements to current light forces in this area, the latter considerably more than the former. To some extent, path 2 might actually reduce the level of threat that could be addressed, since "reachback" weapons involved in the concept leverage precision-guided weapons and, thus, tend to be less appropriate for handling threats other than massed armor, such as infantry-based threats or enemy forces that can operate with short exposure to top attack weapons.

Responsiveness into theater. Here, path 2 offered substantial improvement over current light airborne forces because of the proposed force's smaller overall size and weight. Path 1 mimics current airborne responsiveness, while path 3 would most likely result in a force that has greater airlift burden and, thus, longer timelines into theater. Then again, once in theater, the path 3 force would minimize one of the major shortfalls of today's light units—a lack of tactical mobility and protection. Current light forces cannot fully exploit successes of indirect-fire systems by applying maneuver to decisively defeat an enemy. The advanced maneuvering force would take maximum advantage of innovations as they emerge—directed-energy weapons, ubiquitous sensing, hybrid (powered and/or buoyant) airlifters, robotic vehicles, stealth treatments, etc. It could also streamline the vertical organization of today's forces, from one where information and commands tend to move up and down many echelons to one that is more horizontal, resulting in faster response and greater efficiency in calls for fire.

Beyond these force effectiveness implications, the three paths also have different implementation implications, including the *cost* of creating and maintaining the unit, the *schedule* or time required to develop and train the force, and the *risk* associated with acquiring the new capabilities. Ultimately, such fiscal constraints will help to determine which, if any, paths are taken.

Not surprisingly, path 1 seems the easiest path to implement. As an enhancement of current light airborne forces with a new concept and associated technologies, it has the fewest structural implications. However, while structure would change very little, resources would have to be reallocated to buy the new weapons and RSTA systems the path requires.

Path 2 would require modest changes that would involve reorganizing at least a portion of today's light units. Regular training on the more dispersed tactics and reliance on indirect-fire reachback systems would be key. The Army could either reorganize one or more of its light divisions (including the 82nd Airborne) to achieve the capabilities called for or create new light units of battalion or greater size located at corps level. The latter possibility would require a "bill payer" in terms of manpower and structure. Also, the Army may have to eliminate or truncate other modernization programs to free resources to acquire the systems required for this form of operations. Finally, the type of light force called for would probably have to rely heavily on both overhead sensing and Navy and Air Force reachback fires. Thus, the modernization programs of those services would be particularly important.

Path 3 would be the most capital-intensive course of action because it requires developing and fielding new light- or medium-weight combat vehicles, along with changes to organization, tactics, training, and support. The overall cost would depend highly on the number of units created. For example, if the

Army chose to convert two armored cavalry regiments, the resource implications would be considerably less than to convert the 82nd Airborne, 10th Mountain, and 25th Light Infantry.

Developing a Strategy to Improve Rapid-Reaction Capability

Each of the three paths explored offers both relative strengths and relative weaknesses over a current-day light airborne force, as well as different implementation challenges. In many ways, these dissimilar concepts have characteristics that complement each other. A capability designed for meeting the wide range of tomorrow's rapid-reaction challenge might take on a form that embodies all three paths, provided affordability issues can be resolved. For the foreseeable future, the Army cannot count on any significant increase in either its budget or force structure. Thus, any combination of paths would likely require the Army to reprioritize its resources. In particular, programs that aim to strengthen the "counteroffensive" capability of today's heavy-mechanized forces might have to be weighed with respect to bringing such new capabilities on line. In addition, programs of other services, such as fighter improvements, carrier developments, and ballistic missile defense, may all be less necessary with a more capable rapid-reaction force.

If all three paths were pursued, the notional rapid-reaction capability would consist of three components: (1) a stealthy, small, and very-fast-deploying force that would rely on nonorganic fire support, (2) an enhanced airborne force similar to the 82nd DRB that would be equipped with substantial organic precision fires, and (3) a mounted force equipped with highly agile maneuvering vehicles that can provide both indirect- and direct-fire capability. By our assessment, the technology either already exists or can be developed to create all three components. In fact, although the end capabilities of the components differ, the underlying tactics and technologies would have considerable overlap, possibly yielding an economies of scale effect.

Regardless of what strategy is developed, the capability chosen will need to accommodate future trends. For example, global urbanization trends ensure that MOUT will be an increasingly likely prospect for ground forces. Unless proper decisions are made in terms of equipment, training, and organization, U.S. rapid-reaction forces could see many of their advantages in technology and technique diminished in a MOUT environment. New operational concepts, such as focusing on standoff fires, sealing off areas, and using unmanned systems to help deal with the unique conditions of urban operations, will need to be considered. In addition, the potential difficulties of operations in heavily forested or jungle areas should be considered in developing any new capability.

Many of the sensors and weapons in which U.S. forces are placing great stock can be either severely degraded or even negated in heavily foliated areas. It is not obvious that technology will be able to quickly overcome this problem, and the enemy will likely capitalize on this weakness. Finally, as changes and enhancements are made to the light forces in coming years, the reality that smaller contingencies and missions involving noncombatants will populate the overall mission spectrum should be appropriately addressed in current planning.

Although the research presented here has addressed a wide range of issues, particularly with force effectiveness, many questions should still be answered as the Army moves toward change. Is technology the primary answer, or will it be the human component (organization, selection, training, and motivation) that makes the difference? Will specialized, uniquely trained units for each type of mission (MOUT, low-intensity conflict, high-intensity warfare) ultimately be needed, or can one or a few types of forces be tailored as necessary? How can multiservice, joint, and coalition operations be linked with new Army concepts, and how can this be facilitated? How will the enemy operate to defeat new innovations, and how can these countermeasures be countered? What is the cost of change, and what is the metric that reflects reduced casualties, better responsiveness, and improved deterrence?

Clearly, many questions must be resolved as the Army transitions to a more responsive force with greater rapid-reaction capability. Some of these questions can benefit from additional study and analysis. Others may require experimentation. Still others may require field-testing, training, and implementation to be fully understood. With regard to becoming more relevant in the new millennium with greater rapid-reaction capability, the Army *is* at a crossroads: the time to select a direction is now.